The Daodejing of Laozi

also known as the
Tao De Ching and Dao Te Jing
by
Lao Tzu

This version by
Bruce McCormick

Edited by
Gayle Rasmussen

Copyright 2011

2nd Edition

Bruce McCormick

All rights reserved. No part of this publication may be reproduced, stored in or on any magnetic media or other storage medium other than in its original form when published, or transmitted in any form or by any means (electronic, mechanical, photocopying, recording or otherwise), or translated into other languages without the prior written permission of the author.

ISBN: 0-6155-4808-3
ISBN-13: 978-0-615-54808-1
LCCN: 2011-918965

Cover art
Copyright 2011
Bruce McCormick

Dedication

Dedicated to Thomas Young. He was a dear friend, gentle soul, wonderful role model, true Renaissance man, and a computer nerd extraordinaire who returned to his source, appropriately enough on 01-11-10 at 01:00.

Suggested First Readings

Each chapter of the Dao is a standalone chapter: they may be read in any order without losing any meaning.

If you are not familiar with the Dao, you may get a better appreciation for the tone and general "feel" of the book by reading the following chapters first (in any order). Although they can be understood at a deeper level, they contain more "general wisdom" without delving into the deeper philosophical meaning of the remaining chapters.

2, 3, 7, 9, 11, 13, 17, 20, 24, 27, 29, 37, 38, 46, 49, 50, 53, 57, 60, 61, 63, 64, 66, 69, 71, 72, 74, 75, 76, 78, 80, 81

Contents

	Page
Preface	iii
Acknowledgments	vi
Introduction	vii
Essential Vocabulary	viii

1 What Is the Dao?......................2
2 Universal Contrasts....................4
3 Keeping the People Content............6
4 The Sourceless Dao....................8
5 Impartiality.........................10
6 Staying in Touch With Your Female Side........12
7 Selfless Action......................14
8 How to Recognize a Daoist............16
9 Moderation..........................18
10 What Is Possible?...................20
11 The Value of Emptiness..............22
12 Distractions from the Way...........24
13 Selflessness........................26
14 In Praise of the Profound Dao.......28
15 That Which Reveals Virtue...........30
16 Returning to the Source.............32
17 Leaders.............................34
18 The Decay of Virtue.................36
19 Return to the Center................38
20 The Wise Don't Seem to Fit In.......40
21 The Nature of the Dao...............42
22 Seeking Humility....................44
23 Oneness.............................46
24 Avoiding Extremes...................48
25 Supremacy of the Dao................50
26 Keeping Track of That Which Matters..........52
27 Using the Dao.......................54
28 Cleave To The Feminine..............56
29 Non-assertion (Wu Wei)..............58
30 A Caveat Concerning War.............60
31 Victory Celebrations Should Be Like A Funeral.62
32 The Uncarved Block..................64
33 The Virtue of Self-knowledge........66
34 Virtues.............................68
35 Intangible..........................70
36 Paradoxes...........................72
37 Administration of the Government....74
38 Attributes of the Wise..............75

39	The Roots of Authority	78
40	Existence in Non-existence	80
41	Sameness in Difference	82
42	Daoist Evolution	84
43	The Universal Application of the Dao	86
44	Precepts	88
45	Serenity	90
46	Moderation of Desire	92
47	Understanding Without Knowledge	94
48	Forgetting Knowledge	96
49	Setting the Example	98
50	The Value of Life	100
51	Virtue's Relationship to the Dao	102
52	Keeping to the Source	104
53	Excesses	106
54	Cultivating Virtue	108
55	Attaining Harmony	110
56	Following the Dao	112
57	Simplicity in Governance	114
58	How the Sage Governs	116
59	Serving Others With Moderation	118
60	On Ruling and Evil	120
61	The Virtue of National Humility	122
62	Practicing the Dao	124
63	Avoiding Problems	126
64	Small Steps	128
65	The Virtue of Simplicity	130
66	Subordinating Yourself	132
67	The Three Treasures	134
68	Matching Virtue to the Dao	136
69	Defending Without Engaging	138
70	Easy, But Difficult	140
71	Knowing Not Knowing	142
72	Respect	144
73	Daring to Act	146
74	Capital Punishment	148
75	Government Interference	150
76	Flexibility Versus Rigidity	152
77	Maintaining Balance	154
78	Paradox of the Weakest and Strongest	156
79	Keeping Your Obligations	158
80	A State of Contentment	160
81	The Wise and Otherwise	162
	Appendix - Original Sources	164

Preface

About the original book

2,500 years ago in China, it is said, a little known public official wrote a book which has been translated more than any other book in the world other than the Bible. This book, The Daodejing (often referred to as just "the Dao") is the basis of much of the Eastern world's philosophical and religious thought. It has been published under various spellings, including "Tao Te Ching", "Dao De Ching", "Dao De Jing", "Tao De King", and "Tao Teh Ching". Various writers have spelled the ascribed original author's name "Lao Tzu", "Laozi", "Laose", et. al.

Why the original book?

The story goes that Laozi did not commit the Dao to writing until the last days of his life. He had tried to spread his philosophy by word-of-mouth, but his contemporaries were unable or unwilling to live by his words and he decided to disappear into the wilderness. So he headed off, mounted atop a water buffalo. He eventually reached a guard gate in a remote mountain pass and the guard at the gate beseeched him to write down his philosophy before he left on his final journey. He supposedly wrote the Dao just before disappearing forever. On the other hand, some researchers have come to the conclusion that Laozi did not write the book at all, or, at best, that he wrote only a part of it and the rest was written by a variety of other writers over a long period of time.

While no one is sure who the actual author was, the wisdom of the text has stood the test of time and that is, after all, the most important issue.

Why this book?

There are probably over 200 different "translations" or "interpretations" (I just refer to them as "versions") of the Dao. So why one more?

I began writing my own version of the Dao in about 1981. I was involved in Daoist Studies at the Daoist Institute in North Hollywood, California and studied the Dao as part of my instruction. Since 1981 I have read over 100 versions of the Dao. This book is the culmination of this reading plus my own life experiences.

There are a lot of differences in the various versions of the Dao, so each one has something to contribute to one's understanding of the text. If you read reviews of the various versions on Amazon.com, you will find that many reviewers mention having multiple copies of the Dao. I imagine they have multiple copies just for this reason.

At his writing, I am 62 years old and I highly doubt that I will ever write another book, so please accept this work for what it is: the work of someone trying to understand and live by the words of others much wiser than himself and wanting to share his understanding with others.

The Buddha said, "Believe nothing, no matter where you read it or who said it, no matter if I have said it, unless it agrees with your own common sense." I can only hope that this version will agree with your own common sense. Because the original text is so cryptic, I have attempted to "hear one word and understand two".

English does not provide a gender-neutral third person, so in order to avoid the he/she, him/her dilemma, I have used various contrivances, some of which are not proper English, but which serve to remove that distraction from the text.

I write in books. I highlight and underline in books. I scribble in the margins of books. I write "Yeah, but", "Wow!", "You've got to be kidding" and "Remember this" in books. To this end, I have included a page for your own thoughts opposite each chapter.

Where the sequence of a list or series of things is not time-sequenced, I have occasionally changed the sequence of the original text in an attempt to enhance readability. For example, I have changed the sequence of the 19th chapter (this example from the Feng-English version) from

It is more important
To see the simplicity,
To realize your true nature,
To cast off selfishness
And temper desire.

to

More importantly
    stay centered,
    temper desire,
    strive for simplicity, and
    embrace selflessness.

                      Bruce McCormick
                            2011

Acknowledgements

My thanks, first of all, to my editor, Gayle Rasmussen, for spending what little free time she has on editing the book. A true wordsmith, her review and input was invaluable.

Thanks, also, to those who took time out of their busy lives to review the book before publication. They were all "locals", some of whom had knowledge of the Dao before reading it and some of whom did not. Their input was valuable in making sure that what I was "putting out there" would be readable and meaningful to both veterans of, and newcomers to, the Dao. Those who reviewed the text are:

   Geoff Sherman
   Jack Meyer
   Shirley Voigt
   Debra Hosseini
   Kurt Muzikar
   Anita Watts
   Linda (I didn't get her last name), whom I met late one night
      at The Coffee Bean and Tea Leaf.

I would also like to thank my original instructors at the Taoist Institute in North Hollywood, California, for introducing me to the Dao. The influence that they had on my life was long lasting and profound.

Thanks for the cover art goes to:
   Qin Bing through
   InkDance Chinese Painting Company
   http://www.inkdancechinesepaintings.com
   Email : info@inkdancechinesepaintings.com

Introduction

Daoism is, quite literally, the "go with the flow" philosophy. Athletes report that they can get "lost" in their sport: they cease being a PARTICIPANT in the sport and they BECOME the sport. This is called the "flow phenomenon". I imagine most of us have experienced the flow phenomenon when we have become so passionately involved in an activity that we have completely lost track of time. I believe this is because, like the athlete, our soul has "become one" with the activity and our soul, being eternal, has no concept of time; it only records growth. Daoist philosophy suggests that you should "become one" with the natural course of things and just "go with the flow".

The three main tenets of Daoism are:
    humility,
    compassion, and
    moderation.

They are also referred to by their synonyms: modesty, kindness, and simplicity (or frugality or the absence of excess), respectively. As to the last tenet, I imagine that means that one should practice moderation in practicing moderation. But if one has been "more" than moderate in some way, does one have to be "less" moderate in some other way to balance it out? I leave that up to the readers to decide for themselves. To get an excellent overview of Daoist philosophy, I strongly suggest the reader pick up a copy of an old "Winnie the Pooh" movie and watch it (to refresh your memory of the characters) and then read *The Tao of Pooh*, by Benjamin Hoff.

Essential Vocabulary

This information would normally be in a glossary at the end of the book, but I feel it is important to set a vocabulary baseline for those new to the Dao.

Dao or Tao or Tau (pronounced "dow") literally means "path" or "way" and can figuratively mean "essential nature", "destiny", "principle", or "true path". It is not generally considered to be a 'name' for a 'thing': it is a reference to the natural order of existence.

De or Teh or Te (pronounced somewhat like today's reply to an obvious question: "Duh") is translated as virtue; inherent character; inner strength; integrity; the virtue or power inherent in a person or thing existing in harmony with the Dao. Synonyms used in the text are "mysterious virtue" and "mystic female" or capitalized as "Virtue".

Ching (pronounced "jing") means canon, great book or classic.

Thus the title can be translated as "Canon of the Path and Virtue". Although it contains essentially two different books or sections, the book is generally referred to as just "The Dao".

A continuing theme in the Dao is wu wei (pronounced "woo we"). Synonyms in the text are "non-action", "effortless effort", and "doing not doing". It means that one should do only those things that can be done without interfering with the natural flow of the universe and without seeming to exert any effort.

"The ten thousand things" are all of the things in the world.

The uncarved block, or pu (pronounced "pew"), is the true, natural state of things without human labels, definitions, prejudices, or interference.

The Dao

1

What Is the Dao?

The dao that can be described is not the Dao.
There are no words to describe it because
    words have limits,
    but the Dao does not.
Its source is unknown,
    but it is the ancestor of the ten thousand things.

Its innermost mysteries can be seen only by those
    with insight unclouded by selfish desires.
Those with vision impaired by selfish desires
    see only its surface reflecting back at them;
    they see only its manifestations.
Both of these observers flow from the same source and
    may appear the same,
    but the results they achieve are infinitely different.
This same source is darkness,
    but within the darkness only the selfless one
    will find the gateway to enlightenment.

Thoughts

2

Universal Contrasts

All can see beauty as beauty only because there is ugliness.
All can know good as good only because there is evil.

In the same Way:
    high and low are found side by side;
    difficult and easy coexist effortlessly;
    before and after occur simultaneously;
    being and not being give birth to one another;
    long and short are a measurement of one another;
    soprano and bass experience their highs and lows together.

The Way of the wise is to do only that which needs to be done and
    not to interfere with the natural course of things.

They teach by example,
    not by words.

They encounter things along their Way and they embrace them;
    things leave and they let them go their own Way.

They have without possessing and
    act without expectation.

That which they accomplish they do not hold to themselves,
    yet that which they accomplish is seldom known to others.

The wise accomplish what needs to be done,
    but they accept no credit.
Because they accept no credit,
    credit can never be taken away.

Thoughts

3

Keeping the People Content

If those who are praiseworthy are shown no preference,
    people will cease to be envious.
If possessions are not valued highly,
    people will have no desire to steal them.
If there is nothing that arouses passion,
    people will remain content.

Therefore the truly wise lead by:
    promoting open-mindedness and inner strength;
    emptying minds of knowledge and hearts of desires;
    filling spirits with humility and cores with Virtue.

The wise prefer simplicity and avoid radical ideas;
    thus the foolish intellectuals have no arguments to obstruct them.

The wise work serenely with inner quiet.

They do without doing,
    and thus all turns out well.

Thoughts

4

The Sourceless Dao

The Dao is an empty vessel, yet it is continuously poured from;
    continuously poured from, yet never needing to be refilled.

It is the ultimate source of the ten thousand things.

The Dao
    softens glare,
    blunts sharpness,
    calms disturbances, and
    organizes confusion.

It is like a bottomless pool
    fed by an unknown and never diminishing source.

Whose child it is we do not know, but
    it is the ancestor of the ten thousand things.

Thoughts

5

Impartiality

To the Dao, the ten thousand things are merely effigies:
    each is created for a purpose,
    honored briefly,
    then destroyed.

To the wise, people are the same:
    all appear,
    perform their parts, and
    then vanish.

As effigies represent their worldly counterparts,
    the things of the world represent the Dao.

The universe is like a bellows:
    empty, yet full;
    the more it is emptied,
        the more it yields.

The more you talk of it,
    the less you understand.

Stay centered.

Keep your thoughts within.

Thoughts

6

Staying in Touch With Your Female Side

The spirit of yin is ever present.
It is the mystic female from whom all enduring things originate.
From its mystery, the clearest answers arise.
Although it appears empty, it can never be exhausted.

To acknowledge her presence within you and to use her
    is to do with effortless effort.

Thoughts

7

Selfless Action

The heavens and the earth are ageless.

They constantly change,
    yet are constantly perfect.

They grow and escape confining limitations.

Why is this so?
Because the heavens and the earth live not for themselves.

Therefore, the wise go beyond themselves:
    content to be last,
        they are therefore first;
    being indifferent to themselves,
        they are therefore self-confident;
    being detached from their own images,
        they are therefore one with all things.

Through selfless action,
    the self is fulfilled.

Thoughts

8

How to Recognize a Daoist

The highest motive is to be like water.
It gladly gathers in the low places disdained by others.
It effortlessly nourishes the ten thousand things,
    yet neither attempts to control them
      nor proclaim its own importance.
Rather it is content to seek the lowest level and
    in so doing is like the Dao.

Those who live with the Dao live simply and in harmony with nature.
Their rulings are just.
Their speech is sincere.
Their thoughts are deep.
Their actions are well-timed.
Their relationships are gentle.
They accept things graciously.
Their leadership is egalitarian.
They bind themselves to nothing and seek harmony with all.
Their business dealings are accomplished with quiet efficiency.

Rocks are hard and unyielding.
The stream flows serenely around them and proceeds.

Thoughts

9

Moderation

People are possessed by that which they would possess.
One who knows that enough is enough
    will always have enough.
To take all that you want is never as good as
    to stop when you have all that you need.

It is easier to carry a cup that is half full
    than one that is filled to the brim.
Pull a bowstring too far
    and you will wish you had let go sooner.
Hone a sword's edge too sharp
    and the edge will too soon be worn dull.
Fill your house with gold
    and you invite thieves.
Boastfully proclaim your good fortune
    and you announce your own downfall.

When you attain your goal,
    seek no credit and be satisfied to go no further.

This is the Way of the Dao.

Thoughts

10

What Is Possible?

Can you live your life
    so that it never strays from the Dao?
Can you control your breathing
    so that it is gentle like that of a newborn child?
Can you cleanse your soul
    so that it approaches purity?
Can you love all people, lead them,
    and yet not impose your will?
Can you, as you pass from this earthly existence,
    remain passive and serene?
Can you let all things go their own Way
    without interfering?

Having yet not possessing,
Parenting yet not coddling,
Leading yet not controlling,
Producing yet not taking credit;
This is the mysterious virtue.

Thoughts

11

The Value of Emptiness

The spokes of a wheel are all attached to the hub,
    but it is the emptiness of the hub at its center
    that makes it useful.

Clay can be shaped into a beautiful vessel,
    but it is the empty space within the vessel
    that makes it useful.

Walls, doors, and windows are built to create a building,
    but it is the empty space within the building
    that makes it useful.

Thus, appearance comes from what can be seen;
    value often comes from what cannot.

Therefore, be the space at the center.
Be nothing and you will have everything to give to others.

Thoughts

12

Distractions from the Way

Too many colors distract the eye.
Too many sounds confuse the ear.
Too many tastes mislead the palate.
Too many worldly goods clutter one's Path.
Too many meaningless activities dull one's ability to think clearly.

The wise understand the true significance of things and
    are not distracted or manipulated
    by the illusions that they project;
    they see with their inner eye and
    are not fooled by their physical eyes.

They seek that which is true and ignore that which is false.

Thoughts

13

Selflessness

Both honor and disgrace cause tension.
Those who are honored are tense
> for fear of losing that which has been gained.
Those who are disgraced are tense
> lamenting that which has been lost.

If one accepts being unimportant,
> then gain and loss in worldly things have no meaning.

Since both good fortune and misfortune upset the natural balance,
> the wise see both as unnatural.

Misfortune is caused by selfishness.
If one is selfless, there is no place for misfortune to enter.

When you see the world as part of yourself,
> you will take care of the world.

When you see yourself as part of the world,
> you will take care of yourself.

Thoughts

14

In Praise of the Profound Dao

Looked for,
    it cannot be seen.
Listened for,
    it cannot be heard.
Reached for,
    it cannot be felt.
Used,
    it cannot be exhausted.
You can not define it,
    but you can be one with it.

It rises like the sun,
    but does not illuminate.
It sets like the sun,
    but does not obfuscate.
It is infinite,
    yet it is nothing.

Attempt to stand before it,
    you find it has no beginning.
Attempt to follow behind it,
    you find it has no end.

Hold fast to the ancient Dao and
    you may master the present.
Having mastered the present,
    you may understand the origins of the past.

This is the beginning of wisdom.

Thoughts

15

That Which Reveals Virtue

From ancient times the masters of life have been
    silent,
    subtle,
    simple,
    serene, and
    sensible.

Although their wisdom is beyond our comprehension,
    we can observe their appearance:
    opaque, as a muddied stream;
    courteous, as if they were guests;
    cautious, as if crossing a frozen river;
    simple, as an uncarved block of wood;
    yielding, as ice receding when it melts;
    open-minded, as a wide, inviting valley;
    observant, as if there were dangers all around.

Stir muddy water and it will remain cloudy;
    leave it alone and it will become clear.
Let the stream flow and
    it will find its Way.

If one does not know patience,
    one will not know the right time to act.
If one is not able to be still,
    one's actions will have gathered no power.

Thoughts

16

Returning to the Source

Achieve the highest goal by being passive;
    hold close to a state of perfect serenity.
Within the arising of the ten thousand things
    is the seed of their return to their source.

Returning to the common source is serenity:
    it is to realize one's destiny.
To realize one's destiny
    is to be one with the Dao.
To be one with the Dao
    is to be enlightened.

If you do not realize the source, you have no roots and
    you will therefore stumble in confusion and sorrow.
When you realize your humble beginnings,
    you naturally become humble.

Whoever is one with the Dao is open-minded.
To be open-minded is to be impartial.
To be impartial is to be above nations and laws.
To be above nations and laws is to be in accord with nature.
To be in accord with nature is to be in accord with the Dao.
To be in accord with the Dao is to be eternal.

Though your physical self ends,
    you shall not perish.

Thoughts

17

Leaders

As for the best leaders,
> their people are barely aware of them.

The next best,
> their people honor and praise them.

The next,
> their people fear them.

The last,
> their people despise them.

If you have no faith in your people,
> your people will have no faith in you and
> you will have to resort to laws.

A great leader takes no credit for their work.
When a great leader's work is done,
> the leader's people say, "We did it all by ourselves!"

Thoughts

18

The Decay of Virtue

When the Way is lost,
    morality is born.

When cleverness comes to the leaders,
    hypocrisy takes charge.

When honesty arrives,
    deceit is close behind.

When strengths are recognized,
    weaknesses are exploited.

When respect is elevated,
    arrogance arises.

When kindness is admired,
    cruelty becomes common.

When loyalty is rewarded,
    treachery spreads.

When family relationships disintegrate,
    filial piety is demanded.

When the country begins falling into chaos,
    the government must find enemies to blame.

A nation of heroes
    is a nation in trouble.

Thoughts

19

Return to the Center

Do away with knowledge and
> the people will remember all they need to know.

Do away with morality and righteousness and
> the people will rediscover compassion and duty.

Do away with profit and greed and
> there will be no desire for thieving and robbing.

These are all only visible signs.

More importantly,
> stay centered;
> temper desire;
> strive for simplicity;
> embrace selflessness.

Thoughts

20

The Wise Don't Seem to Fit In

Renounce knowledge and
    you may begin to understand.

Is the difference between "yes" and "no" as important as
    the difference between "good" and "evil"?
Must one value what others value?
Of course not!

Others seem to know their purpose in life;
    the wise seem to drift as a homeless waif.
Others seem to have more than they need;
    the wise seem to have nothing considered of value.
Others seem to have immediate answers;
    the wise apparently do not even understand the questions.
Others claim to be intelligent and gifted;
    the wise appear ignorant and out of step.
Others are constantly busy;
    the wise seem aimless and without purpose.

Alone, the wise seem ignorant and dull.
The wise are nourished by the mystic female.

Thoughts

21

The Nature of the Dao

The Dao is like a dream:
    invisible,
    intangible, and
    obscure.

It is invisible,
    yet it has form.
It is intangible,
    yet there is a feel to it.
Its ways are obscure,
    yet there is a method to them.
Since there is a method to them,
    there are signs of them.

From ancient times and by many names it has been known.
How can one know this is true?
By looking inside one's self!

Thoughts

22

Seeking Humility

If you wish to become whole,
    first become broken.
If you wish to become straight,
    first become bent.
If you wish to become full,
    first become empty.
If you wish to become renewed,
    first become worn out.

Have little and you will have enough.
Have abundance and you will have trouble.

Thus, the wise embrace oneness with the Dao and
    show the Way for all.

Not displaying themselves,
    they are a shining example.
Not justifying themselves,
    they are believed.
Not boasting,
    they are recognized.
Not seeking glory,
    they are respected.
Not seeking power,
    they are leaders.

Thus, it is as the ancients said:
    "Yield and overcome."
    "Be empty and be full."
    "Give up everything and you will have all that you need."

Let your deeds remain a secret
    and the results will speak for themselves.

Thoughts

23

Oneness

Nature is sparing in its conversation.
Though a gale blows,
>   it will only last a short time.
A cloudburst lasts only until
>   the cloud is spent of its water.
If the heavens and the earth cannot sustain such activity,
>   how can you?

If you are one with the Dao,
>   the Dao welcomes you.
If you are one with Virtue,
>   Virtue is always there with you.
If you are one with both,
>   then harmony and equilibrium will exist in your life.
If you are not one with either,
>   then you will become lost
>   and confusion will rule your heart.

One who does not trust will not be trusted.

Therefore, seek only to become a vessel empty of yourself,
>   filled with oneness.

Thoughts

24

Avoiding Extremes

Those who seek glory are not true leaders.
Those who are self-righteous will be ignored.
Those who boast are proclaiming their own failure.
Those who stand on tiptoe are not firmly grounded.
Those who try to outshine others dim their own light.
Those who walk with long strides will soon fall behind.

To the followers of the Dao,
    these are excess food and baggage.
As such, they are to be avoided.

Thoughts

25

Supremacy of the Dao

Before the universe was born,
> in the silent center of the whirling winds of change,
>> something invisible appeared.

Without voice, it created countless sounds.
Without motion, it produced unceasing activity.
Without form, it gave birth to the ten thousand things.

I do not know its name.
If I must name it,
> I call it the Dao, the Path to life.

Being the Path to life,
> it is a long road.
Being long,
> it reaches out a great distance.
Reaching out a great distance,
> it returns to its origin.

Thus the Dao is great,
> the universe is great,
> the earth is great, and
> human beings are great.

Human beings are subject to the laws of earth,
> earth is subject to the laws of the universe,
> the universe is subject to the laws of the Dao, and
> the Dao is subject to its own nature.

Thoughts

26

Keeping Track of That Which Matters

As heavy is the foundation of the light,
    so serenity is the master of passion.

Therefore, the sage, traveling all day in his cart,
    does not lose track of his most important possessions.

Though there be many magnificent distractions,
    the sage remains simple, serene and passive.
For how can one who rules ten thousand chariots
    for one moment relax his vigil?
If he is too light-hearted,
    discipline is lost.
If he is too restless,
    serenity is lost.

Thoughts

27

Using the Dao

A good trader needs no scales.
A good traveler leaves no tracks.
A good door remains shut without a latch.
A good knot will not come undone by itself.
A good speaker leaves no grounds for rebuttal.

The sage is willing to help all of creation;
> the sage does not abandon even the smallest creature.

This is called enlightenment.

What is a good person?
> A teacher of bad people.

What is a bad person?
> A good person's raw material.

If the teacher is not respected by the student or
> the student is not cared for by the teacher,
> confusion and dissension will arise.

This is an essential teaching of the Dao.

Thoughts

28

Cleave to the Feminine

There is nothing stronger than gentleness.
There is nothing more gentle than true strength.
Understand and use the energy and strength
> of the masculine when necessary,
>> but cleave to the feminine.

Be aware of the light, but keep to the darkness,
> and you will be an example to the world.

Teach the truth by living it.
Achieve the highest,
> but appear the lowest.

Acknowledge honors,
> but remain humble.

Just as all streams descend into the valley,
> all things come to those who open themselves.

The uncarved block can be made into any number of tools.
The wise create only those tools required to lead,
> but their tools are never ends in themselves.

Thus, "a great tailor cuts little".

Thoughts

29

Non-assertion (Wu Wei)

Do you believe that you can improve the whole world?
I do not believe that it can be done.

The ten thousand things are continually changing,
    yet they are always exactly as they should be.
They cannot be improved with your small efforts.
With larger efforts, they can be ruined.

The earth is a sacred vessel.
If you try to use it,
    you may crush it.
If you try to change it,
    it may shatter.
If you let it go,
    it will remain useful.
If you leave it alone,
    it will change for you.

Force yourself ahead,
    and you will later be left behind.

Take more than your share,
    and you will later have less than enough.

Overexert yourself,
    and you will later become weak.

Therefore, the sage keeps to the center and
    avoids extremes and excesses.

Thoughts

30

A Caveat Concerning War

To those who would counsel leaders in the Way of the Dao,
    advise them not to attempt to conquer the world.
For where armies have marched,
    thorns and briers thrive.
Where a great army has advanced,
    hunger and evil follow.

Once the wise have attained their purpose,
    they stop at that.
They win because they must,
    but not by force or violence.
Their victory once made,
    they understand that arrogance may be the next enemy.
They will not press for further victory,
    for victors are by victory undone.
They do not boast, celebrate or revel in the spoils.
They understand that vengeance is a vessel with a hole
    that carries nothing but the promise of emptiness.

Use of force is followed by loss of strength.
This is not following the Dao.

Thoughts

31

Victory Celebrations Should Be Like A Funeral

Weapons are instruments of fear, violence, and evil.
Followers of the Dao use them only with calm and restraint and
    only when they have no other choice.

Those who value peace do not honor killing;
    they enter battle with great sorrow and compassion.

Those who do not mourn the killing of even one person
    have lost their Way.
Those who delight in the killing of anything
    have lost their oneness with all things.

Those who do not value peace
    oppose the laws of nature.
If peace is their true objective,
    then victory is no cause for rejoicing.

Thus, upon winning a war, one should celebrate by mourning.

Thoughts

32

The Uncarved Block

The Dao eternal has no name.
Though it appears small and insignificant,
    there is no container large enough to contain it.

An uncarved block, though small,
    contains more potential than a beautifully carved sculpture.
If leaders could harness that potential:
    The Dao would reign on earth;
    gentle rain would fall equally to all people;
    the ten thousand things would live in harmony;
    people would need no written laws
        because they would follow their own Way naturally.

When the uncarved block is cut,
    names begin.
As soon as there are names,
    one ought to know that too much has been done.
Whoever knows this is free from danger.

The Dao in the world is like a river
    flowing on its Way through the valley.

Thoughts

33

The Virtue of Self-knowledge

One who knows others is wise.
One who knows the self is enlightened.

One who masters others is strong.
One who masters the self has true strength.

One who is content is wealthy.
One who perseveres has inner strength.

One who accepts their place amongst the ten thousand things
    will endure.
One who embraces death shall not perish,
    but shall be eternally present.

Thoughts

34

Virtues

The great Dao flows unabated in all directions.

The life of the ten thousand things depend upon it,
    but it exercises no authority.

It provides for everything,
    yet it lays claim to nothing.

Since it is without desires,
    it is humble.

Being the source of the ten thousand things,
    all things seek it out for refuge,
        yet it does not seek to master or control anything.

Because it never proclaims its own greatness,
    it is truly great.

Thoughts

35

Intangible

When you are one with the Dao,
      you may roam where you will with no evil to fear:
      calm, peaceful, and at ease.

Music and good food persuade the passing traveler to stop.
But a discussion of the Dao given in passing
      will seem unappealing and tasteless.

Looked for, it cannot be seen.
Listened for, it cannot be heard.
Used, it cannot be exhausted.

Thoughts

36

Paradoxes

That which is to weaken
    must first be strengthened.
That which is to be taken away
    must first be bestowed.
That which is to become smaller
    must first be enlarged.
That which is to be uprooted
    must first be allowed to grow.

This is subtle enlightenment.

The soft and pliable will overcome the hard and inflexible.

Just as fish should remain safely hidden in the deep waters,
    the nation's weapons should remain safely out of sight.

Thoughts

37

Administration of the Government

The Dao does nothing merely for the sake of doing it.

It never interferes,
    yet there is nothing it does not do.

If all leaders abided by this,
    the ten thousand things would develop naturally,
    each according to its own Way.

Should the leaders feel compelled to act,
    the wise would have them return
    to the simplicity of the uncarved block.

In the simplicity of the uncarved block there is no desire.
With no desire there is no expectation.
With no expectation there is no disappointment.
With no disappointment there is serenity.

Thoughts

38

Attributes of the Wise

One who is good is not aware of their goodness,
    and is therefore good.
One who is foolish claims to be good,
    and is therefore not good.

One who is wise appears to do nothing,
    yet leaves nothing undone.
One who is foolish is always busy,
    yet accomplishes little.

One who is wise hears one word,
    yet understands two.
One who is foolish hears two words,
    yet understands only one,
    but believes they understand three.

When the Dao is lost, righteousness appears.
When righteousness disappears, obedience is demanded.
When obedience declines, regulations arise.
When regulations are ignored, force begins.
When force begins, disorder, chaos and death rule the land.

If you are not one with the Dao,
    your knowledge comes from your own misunderstanding;
    it is the flower of your folly.

The truly wise seek the center, not the surface;
    they take the fruit, and leave the flower.
Therefore, they use only what is usable today,
    and leave tomorrow's fruit for tomorrow.

Thoughts

39

The Roots of Authority

The ten thousand things have from ancient times sought unity with the Dao:
    the heavens attained it and became clear;
    the earth attained it and became firm;
    the valleys attained it and became fertile;
    the spirit attained it and became inspired;
    the wise attained it and became leaders.

Without clarity,
    the heavens would be poisonous.
Without firmness,
    the earth would tremble.
Without fertility,
    the valleys would become arid.
Without inspiration,
    the spirit would be lost.
Without leaders,
    good nations would falter and fail.

Thus good leaders are humble.
The high are dependent upon the low for support.
Leaders speak of themselves as
    "orphans", "virtueless", and "unworthy".
Does this not indicate that they must depend upon humility
    to gain the support of the people?

Those who are one with the Dao seek not to shine
    as an overvalued gem,
    but rather seek to be seen as an unpretentious stone.

Thoughts

40

Existence in Non-existence

The Dao is an endless circle with serenity as its ultimate function.

The ten thousand things arise from what-is.
What-is arose from what-is-not.

From absolute nothing comes everything.

Thoughts

41

Sameness in Difference

The wise hear of the Dao and practice it diligently.
The indifferent hear of the Dao and are aware of it,
    but neither understand nor practice it.
The foolish hear of the Dao and laugh out loud.

Without the foolish laughter,
    the Dao would not be as significant as it is.

Hence it is said:
    the highest virtue seems corrupt;
    going forward seems like retreat;
    the perfect sound can not be heard;
    the purest innocence seems polluted;
    the brightest path seems the most dim;
    the squarest square has no square corners;
    substantial worth seems like shifting tides.

The Way is unmarked and unnamed.
The Dao fulfills everything that stays on its Path.

Thoughts

42

Daoist Evolution

The Dao begot one.
One begot two.
Two begot three.
Three begot the ten thousand things.

The ten thousand things benefit from emphasizing yin
     and acknowledging yang.
From their blending together,
     balance and harmony exist in the universe.
Truly then, one gains by losing, and loses by gaining.

I teach what others also teach:
     "A person of violence will find a violent end."

This is the essence of my teaching.

Thoughts

43

The Universal Application of the Dao

The softest will penetrate the hardest.
That which offers no contention can enter
    where there appears to be no opening.
This is why the wise know the benefit of doing not-doing.

Those who can teach without words will not be disputed with
    by those who hear only words.
Those who can achieve without effort will not be opposed
    by those who understand only force.

The wise become silent and invisible.
Being silent and invisible,
    they are not interfered with.

Thoughts

44

Precepts

Fame or self: which is more dear?
Wealth or self: which is more prized?
Gain or loss: which is more painful?

One who looks outside of their self for fulfillment
    will seek in vain.
One who hoards
    will suffer heavy loss.

One who is content
    is not subject to harmful extremes.
One who practices doing not-doing
    does not continue on into trouble.

Thoughts

45

Serenity

The most perfect seems imperfect,
    but it endures because it is one with itself.
The greatest fullness seems empty,
    but it is inexhaustible.

The most wise seems foolish.
The most skilled seems clumsy.
The most straight seems crooked.
The most eloquent seems tongue-tied.

While stillness overcomes heat and
    physical activity overcomes cold,
        the serene and passive are the universal ideals.

Thoughts

46

Moderation of Desire

When the leaders work with the Dao
    horses fertilize the fields and there is food.
When the leaders work against the Dao
    horses are trained for war and there is starvation.

The greatest curse is having desires;
    it is the greatest misery.
The greatest sin is selfish striving.

Contentment is not found in obtaining all that one wants.
It is found in the realization of how much one already has.
Being content with contentment is to be always content.

Thoughts

47

Understanding Without Knowledge

One can know the world without going outside.
One can find the Dao without even looking outside.
The further you go outside looking for knowledge,
    the further you will be from understanding.

Accordingly, the sage:
    does without doing,
    sees without looking, and
    understands without knowledge.

Thoughts

48

Forgetting Knowledge

On the way to knowledge,
    much is accumulated.
On the Way to wisdom,
    much is discarded.

Less and less is done,
    until not-doing is done.
And when not-doing is done,
    nothing is left undone.

The best rulers rule by letting things follow their own Path.
Interfering only complicates the job of ruling.
Interfering only disrupts the natural balance.

Thoughts

49

Setting the Example

The wise are selfless;
They worry only about fulfilling the needs of others.

The good are treated with goodness.
The bad are also treated with goodness.
In so doing, goodness is gained.

The faithful are treated with faith.
The unfaithful are also treated with faith.
In so doing, faith is gained.

The trustworthy are treated with trust.
The untrustworthy are also treated with trust.
In so doing, trust is gained.

The compassionate are treated with compassion.
The compassionless are also treated with compassion.
In so doing, compassion is gained.

For good, return good.
For an injustice, return only justice.
For a wrong, repay with forgiveness.
For a kindness, repay only with kindness.

The wise are shy and humble.
To the world they seem confused,
    but people watch them and listen to them.

The wise behave as little children
    and treat all things as their children.

Thoughts

50

The Value of Life

The moment people come into life
    they begin to die.

Three out of ten are one with life
    because they are afraid of death.
Three out of ten are one with death
    because they are afraid to live.
Three out of ten are one with neither life nor death
    and find an early death by foolishly living life.

Why is this?
Because none of them are one with both life and death.

The tenth, the one who remains on the Path,
    is one with both life and death.

It is said that they
    are not attacked by wild animals and
    are not vulnerable on the field of battle.

    Wild animals are not threatened by them and
    opposing forces do not recognize them as an enemy.

Why is this?
Because they are one with all things,
    all things see them as one of their own.

Fear not death,
    but fear that by the time you die you have not lived.

Thoughts

51

Virtue's Relationship to the Dao

While all things arise from the Dao,
    they are protected and nourished by the mystic female.

They are formed from matter and
    shaped by their environment.

Thus, the ten thousand things naturally respect the Dao
    and honor the mystic female.
This respect and honor are not required,
    but they come naturally to all things
    if they are not interfered with.

The Dao creates without claiming ownership,
    does without taking credit, and
    guides without interfering.

This is the Mystic Power.

Thoughts

52

Keeping to the Source

The beginning of the universe may be considered its mother.
Knowing the mother,
    the children can be known.
Knowing the children,
    you may remain close to the mother.
Remaining close to the mother,
    you will not meet with danger.

The undiscerning mind is like the roots of a tree:
    it absorbs equally from all that touches it,
    even the poison that would kill it.
Quiet your senses to avoid temptations
    that lead you away from the Dao.
Eyes closed, mouth shut,
    life is without trouble.
Eyes open, mouth busy,
    life is without hope.

Whoever yields has the most strength.
Whoever does not judge shall not be judged.
Whoever is enlightened has the brightest vision.
Whoever sees their own insignificance sees most clearly.

This is following the Dao.

Thoughts

53

Excesses

The Way is easy,
    but rocky paths are popular.

If the palace gardens are well manicured
    but the farmers' fields are overgrown with weeds,
        then too soon the palace pantries will be empty.

If the palace pantries are full
    but the farmers' granaries are empty,
        then too soon there will be no bread at the palace.

If the swords of the palace guards are well sharpened
    but there is no fuel to fire the forge of the blacksmith,
        then too soon the palace will lack sufficient defenses.

If the palace dwellers are elegantly dressed
    but the peasants lack material to repair their own garments,
        then too soon the palace dwellers will be without
        elegant clothes.

Are the palace dwellers not wasteful robbers?
Have they not departed from the Dao?

Thoughts

54

Cultivating Virtue

That which is firmly planted
    is not easily uprooted.
That which is firmly grasped
    does not easily slip loose.
Those who do things well
    will be honored by their descendants.

Accept the Dao in yourself
    and Virtue is yours.
Accept the Dao in the family
    and Virtue is abundant.
Accept the Dao in the village
    and Virtue multiplies.
Accept the Dao in the nation
    and Virtue flourishes.
Accept the Dao in the world
    and Virtue is universal.

Therefore, one can measure by the accumulated Virtue:
By your Virtue,
    gauge the family;
By the family's Virtue,
    gauge the village;
By the village's Virtue,
    gauge the nation;
By the nation's Virtue,
    gauge the world.

How does one know this is so?
It is self-evident!

Thoughts

55

Attaining Harmony

Whoever is filled with Virtue is like a child:
    They are one with all things,
        so all things see them as one of their own;
    They are soft and weak,
        but their grasp is firm and strong;
    They are not consumed with the union of man and woman,
        so their vital energy is not diminished;
    They can shout all day,
        but not become hoarse.

This is being in harmony with the Dao.
Being in harmony with the Dao is to know the eternal.
To know the eternal is to be enlightened.

To become excitable leads to confusion.
Things reach their prime and then decline.
To freely vent emotions is to be aggressive.
To unnaturally attempt to extend life is unnatural.

To be impatient is to oppose the Dao.
Whatever opposes the Dao soon ceases to exist.

Thoughts

56

Following the Dao

One who knows does not necessarily speak.
One who speaks does not necessarily know.
Keep your mouth closed.

Simplify your life.
Mask your brilliance.
Blunt your sharpness.
Be one with the dust of the earth.
Be careful about what you absorb from the world.

This is being one with the Dao.

Be like the Dao:
    it can not be benefited or harmed;
    it can not be honored or disgraced;
    it can not be approached or withdrawn from.
It gives itself up continually,
    therefore it endures.

This is the highest human state.

Thoughts

57

Simplicity in Governance

Laws may govern a state,
    but empires are kept alive the longest
    by doing only those things that are required to rule and
    no more.

How can we know this is true?

Regulations are written "to guide the people".
The more regulations that are passed,
    the more criminals you create.

Weapons are accumulated "to protect the people".
The more weapons there are,
    the more threats and dangers arise.

Officials are appointed "to serve the people".
The more clever the officials are,
    the more confusion rules the land.

Taxes are passed "to provide for the people".
The more taxes there are
    the more poverty increases.

Religions are espoused "to make the people more tolerant".
The more religion there is,
    the more intolerance and prejudice there is.

Without too many regulations, there may honesty.
Without too many weapons, there may be peace.
Without clever officials, there may be order.
Without onerous taxes, there may be wealth.
Without religious intolerance, there is acceptance.

As government influence increases,
    freedom and initiative are taken away.

Thoughts

58

How the Sage Governs

Govern passively,
> the people are happy.
Govern with severity,
> the people become treacherous.

Disaster arises from good fortune.
Good fortune arises from disaster.

When the state is self-righteous,
> self-righteousness becomes strategy and
> good becomes evil.

Therefore, the rule of the sage is:
> sharp, but not cutting;
> bright, but not blinding;
> assertive, but not aggressive;
> to the point, but not obnoxious.

Thoughts

59

Serving Others With Moderation

By practicing moderation,
    an abundance of Virtue is accumulated over time.
With sufficient Virtue,
    one gains sovereignty over the self.
With sovereignty over the self,
    nothing is impossible.
If nothing is impossible,
    one has no limits.
If one has no limits,
    they are fit to lead a nation.

With this mother principle of power,
    one's rule may be long and beneficial to all.

This is called having deep roots and a strong trunk.
This is the key to a long life and understanding the eternal.

Thoughts

60

On Ruling and Evil

Rule a great state as you would cook a small fish:
>too much poking and it will fall apart.

Evil can not be conquered in the world;
>it can only be resisted within one's self.

Rule with the Dao
>and evil spirits will lose their potency.

Evil spirits will still have power,
>but they will not harm the people.

If you give evil nothing to oppose,
>then it will disappear out of boredom.

Thoughts

61

The Virtue of National Humility

A great nation is like a valley through which streams descend.
It is the meeting place, the female, of the world,
    quietly and passively overcoming the male
    by humble submission.

If a great nation humbly lowers itself beneath a smaller nation,
    it may win the allegiance of the smaller;
If a smaller nation humbly accepts its status beneath the greater,
    it may win the allegiance of the greater.
Therefore, some lower themselves to win others;
    some are already low, and therefore win others.

When both countries humbly submit,
    then both countries can benefit greatly.

Thoughts

62

Practicing the Dao

The Dao is the source of the ten thousand things.
It is the sage's best friend
    and the bad person's nemesis.

Good words win honor in the eyes of others,
    but good deeds win the Dao.

Abandoning the misguided without helping them find their Way
    will take you far from the Dao.

Therefore, when new leaders are installed into office,
    do not bring them extravagant gifts;
        bring instead the Dao as your tribute.

Why was the Dao so valued by the ancients?
Because if you are one with the Dao,
    when you seek, you find;
    when you make a mistake, you are forgiven.
Therefore it is the most prized gift in the world.

Thoughts

63

Avoiding Problems

Act by not acting.
Do by not doing.
Strive for effortlessness.

That problem which has not arisen is easily prevented.
Appreciate the plain and simple.

Find solutions to the small problems
    while they are still small.
Find greatness
    by undertaking nothing great.

Anticipate the difficult
    by managing the easy.
Undertake the difficult
    before it becomes more difficult.
The wise know that things are difficult
    and therefore meet with few difficulties.

The wise never undertake more than can be done
    without doing too much;
    therefore nothing remains undone.

Thoughts

64

Small Steps

That which is tiny is easily lost.
That which is fragile is easily broken.
That which is not moving is easily held.

Prevent trouble before it arises.

A tall building arises from a pile of bricks.
A tree of great girth grows from a tiny sprout.
A journey of a thousand miles begins with a single step.

The wise, because they do not-doing,
    seldom ruin anything.
Because they do not lay hold of anything,
    they lose nothing.
Because they have nothing,
    they have nothing to lose.

In their enterprises, the people generally ruin things
    when on the verge of success.
Be as careful at the end as at the beginning and
    there will be few ruined enterprises.

The sage desires not to desire and
    does not value goods which are difficult to obtain.

Thus the truly wise:
    avoid desires;
    want the unwanted;
    learn to unlearn what has been learned;
    master nature not by conquering it,
        but by becoming one with it.

Thoughts

65

The Virtue of Simplicity

The ancient followers of the Dao did not use it
    to increase the people's knowledge,
    but rather to preserve simplicity.
People are difficult to lead
    when they have too much knowledge.
They will find their own Way naturally
    when they know what they don't know.

Whoever rules a country by furthering knowledge
    is that nation's curse.
Whoever rules a country by furthering simplicity
    is that nation's blessing.
To know these two principles
    is to know the ancient standard.

The mystic female is always found on the Path with the Dao.
In this way, the harmony of the universe is maintained.
If one strays from the Path, they can be one with neither.

Thoughts

66

Subordinating Yourself

Rivers are able to rule the valleys because
    they are willing to take the more humble position.

To be elevated by the people,
    speak as their inferior.
To lead the people,
    put their interests in front of your own.

Thus the truly wise are above,
    but the people do not feel their weight.
They walk in front,
    but the people do not feel blocked.

The whole world respects and
    never grows tired of such leadership.

Because the truly wise do not contend,
    no one can contend against them.

Thoughts

67

The Three Treasures

Many say that following the Dao is the Way of a fool.
If it were not the Way of a fool,
    it would not be so simple.
If it were the way of the learned,
    it would have vanished long ago,
        buried under rules and definitions.

Those recognized as ignorant may lack knowledge,
    but knowledge is not wisdom.
Even the ignorant can understand this,
    yet the learned do not.

There are three treasures which the wise hold and keep.
The first is compassion, from which comes courage.
The second is moderation, from which comes generosity.
The third is humility, from which comes leadership.

You cannot shun compassion and still be brave.
You cannot abandon moderation and still be generous.
You cannot forget humility and still be a leader.

Through compassion,
    one will triumph in attack and
    be impregnable in defense.

What the Dao helps,
    it protects with the gift of compassion.

Thoughts

68

Matching Virtue to the Dao

A good fighter is not angry.
A good warrior is not violent.
A good winner is not boastful.
A good tactician plans to avoid confrontation.

This is known as the virtue of non-contention,
    the virtue of serenity.
This is the mastery of life.
This is matching Virtue to the Dao.

Thoughts

69

Defending Without Engaging

Ancient military strategists said:
    "I would rather be invaded than be the invader."
    "I would rather retreat one foot than advance one inch."

This is called:
    marching without moving,
    being armed with invisible weapons,
    repelling the enemy without using force, and
    defeating the enemy without engaging them.

The greatest strategic mistake is
    underestimating your enemy.
If you underestimate your enemy,
    you may lose everything that you value.

There is no greater offense to the Dao
    than entering a battle with the anticipation of glory.
Battles should be fought only with compassion, humility,
    and sorrow that many will die on both sides.
Thus, when armies meet in battle, victory will go to the one
    that enters with the greatest compassion.

Thoughts

70

Easy, But Difficult

My words are easy to understand and easy to live by,
    yet it appears that few can understand or live by them.
My words come from the ancients and my actions are reasoned,
    but because most do not recognize this,
    I remain little known.

Because so few know and live by my teachings,
    the teachings are even more important.

But honor comes to me when least I'm known.

The sage, carrying a jewel within, wears simple clothes.

Thoughts

71

Knowing Not Knowing

Those who are unafraid to say that they do not know
    may become wise.
Those who insist that they know
    will never understand.

Those who recognize their weaknesses
    may gain strength.
Those who neglect their strengths
    will become weak.

Wisdom and strength
    come from the courage to see things as they are.

Thoughts

72

Respect

If the people fear your power,
    you have none.
If the people do not fear your power,
    you truly have power.

Do not meddle in their personal business or their livelihoods.

If you respect them,
    they will respect you.

The wise know themselves,
    but do not make a show of themselves.
They have self-respect,
    but are not self-important.
They let go of flattery and
    choose regard for the self.

Thoughts

73

Daring to Act

One with courage and passion will kill or be killed.
One with courage, but compassionate, cherishes life.
From these two kinds of courage arise both harm and benefit.

The Dao does not favor some things.
Who knows why?
Even the most wise do not know why.

The Dao:
    does not speak, yet it is answered;
    does not contend, yet it overcomes;
    does not command, yet it is complied with;
    does not ask for anything, yet it receives all it needs;
    is empty, yet it contains the master plan.

The meshes of the Dao's net are wide,
    yet nothing of importance slips through.

Thoughts

74

Capital Punishment

If the people do not fear death,
    why threaten them with it?
If the people do fear death, and if the unlawful be put to death,
    who would dare to execute them?

There is an official executioner.
To try to take the place of the official executioner
    is to allow an unskilled worker
        to wield the hatchet of a master carpenter;
        the worker will rarely escape chopping off their own hand!

Thoughts

75

Government Interference

The people starve
 when rulers gobble up heavy taxes.
The people are rebellious
 when rulers meddle in their affairs.
The people do not fear death
 when the rulers demand too much from life.

Wise rulers do only those things that benefit all of the people,
 then they go away and leave the people alone.

Thoughts

76

Flexibility Versus Rigidity

When living, humans are supple and yielding;
 when dead they are hard and stiff.
When living, plants are soft and pliant;
 when dead they are withered and brittle.
Thus, being inflexible and unyielding is part of dying;
 being flexible and yielding is part of living.

Therefore, an inflexible army will lose in war
 just as an unyielding tree is the first to snap under the axe.

The hard, stiff, and brittle will fail.
The supple and pliant will overcome.

Thoughts

77

Maintaining Balance

Is not the Dao like a drawn bow:
    the lowest part is raised;
    the highest part is lowered;
    the overall length is shortened;
    the overall depth is lengthened?

The Way of the Dao is to remove from where there is excess
    and to add to where there is not enough.
Without the Dao,
    humans do things differently.
They take from those who are lacking
    to give to those who already have more than they can use.

What person has barely enough and yet gives it to the world?
    Only a person on the Path.

Therefore, the wise work without recognition and
    give without expecting anything in return.
They achieve what has to be done without claiming credit and
    do not glory in any praise.

Thoughts

78

Paradox of the Weakest and Strongest

Water is the softest and most yielding thing on earth,
    yet its silken gentleness will eventually wear away
    the hardest stone.

Thus, the weak will overcome the strong and
    the flexible will overcome the rigid.
The whole world can perceive this,
    but few put it into practice.
Those who remain on the Path
    yield and overcome.

And so the truly wise say:
    "Whoever is the lowest servant of the kingdom
        is worthy of becoming its ruler" and
    "Whoever is willing to tackle the most unpleasant tasks
        is the best ruler."

The truth is often paradoxical.

Thoughts

79

Keeping Your Obligations

When peace is made between enemies,
    some animosity is bound to remain not dispelled.

Therefore the wise keep their part of the bargain,
    but do not expect to receive that which is due to them.

One of virtue fulfills their obligations,
    but one without virtue requires others to fulfill theirs.

And so it is truly said:
    "The Dao does not choose sides.
        Those on the Path receive from the Dao
            because they are one with it."

Thoughts

80

A State of Contentment

The ideal country is small and has a small population.
It has an abundance of goods beyond possible use.
The people take death seriously.
Though they have horses, carts and boats,
    they do not travel far from their birthplace.
Though they have weapons,
    they do not display them and
    they use them only for defense.

Let them:
    be satisfied with their food,
    be happy with their customs,
    be attractive in their clothing,
    be comfortable in their homes, and
    use knotted ropes for keeping track.

Though adjoining states are within sight of one another,
    and the sound of barking dogs and crowing roosters in one
        can be heard in the other,
    the people of one state will grow old and die
        without having had any dealings with the other.

Thoughts

81

The Wise and Otherwise

Truthful words are not necessarily eloquent.
Eloquent words are not necessarily truthful.

The wise need not argue.
Those who need to argue are not wise.

The wise are not necessarily learned.
The learned are not necessarily wise.

The wise do not hoard their things.
Having very little left after serving and giving to others,
    they have enough and a little to spare.
But having given all that they have given,
    they are very rich indeed.

The Way of the sage is to do without doing.

The sage benefits everyone and contends with no one.

Thoughts

Appendix

Original Sources

Feng, Guia-fu and Jane English. *Tao Te Ching, A New Translation.* New York: Vintage Books, 1972.

Cheng, Man-Jan. *Lao Tzu: My Words Are Very Easy to Understand.* Richmond, CA: North Atlantic Books, 1981.

Bynner, Witter. *The Way of Life According to Lao Tzu.* New York: Perigee Books, 1972.

Mair, Victor H. *Tao Te Ching: The Classic Book of Integrity and the Way.* New York: Bantam Books, 1990.

Goddard, Dwight and Henri Borel. *Lao Tzu's Tao and Wu Wei.* New York: Brentano, 1919.

www.ingramcontent.com/pod-product-compliance
Lightning Source LLC
Chambersburg PA
CBHW032119040426
42449CB00005B/197